I KNOW THE DAYS OF THE WEEK

By Mary Rose Osburn

Gareth Stevens
PUBLISHING

first concepts

I know the days
of the week.

There are seven days
in a week.

Sunday	Monday	Tuesday	Wednesday

Thursday	Friday	Saturday

Grandpa visits
on Sunday.

We go to the library
on Monday.

We swim
on Tuesday.

We go to the park
on Wednesday.

13

We go to the zoo
on Thursday.

We clean on Friday.

16

17

We play baseball
on Saturday.

19

Then, it is
Sunday again.
Another week begins!

What day of the week
do you like best?

22

Sunday

Monday

Tuesday

Wednesday

Thursday

Friday

Saturday

23

Please visit our website, www.garethstevens.com. For a free color catalog of all our high-quality books, call toll free 1-800-542-2595 or fax 1-877-542-2596.

Cataloging-in-Publication Data

Names: Osburn, Mary Rose.
Title: I know the days of the week / Mary Rose Osburn.
Description: New York : Gareth Stevens Publishing, 2017. | Series: What I know
Identifiers: ISBN 9781482454536 (pbk.) | ISBN 9781482454581 (library bound) | ISBN 9781482454550 (6 pack)
Subjects: LCSH: Time – Juvenile literature. | Days – Juvenile literature. | Week – Juvenile literature.
Classification: LCC QB209.5 O83 2017 | DDC 529'.1–dc23

First Edition

Published in 2017 by
Gareth Stevens Publishing
111 East 14th Street, Suite 349
New York, NY 10003

Designer: Sarah Liddell
Editor: Therese Shea

Photo credits: Cover, p. 1 (stripes) Eky Studio/Shutterstock.com; cover, p. 1 (calendar) Jirsak/Shutterstock.com; p. 3 nukeaf/Shutterstock.com; p. 5 Heath Johnson/Shutterstock.com; pp. 7, 21 VGstockstudio/Shutterstock.com; p. 9 Tyler Olsen/Shutterstock.com; p. 11 wavebreakmedia/Shutterstock.com; p. 13 Jo Ann Snover/Shutterstock.com; p. 15 Robert Pernell/Shutterstock.com; p. 17 PAKULA PIOTR/Shutterstock.com; p. 19 Suzanne Tucker/Shutterstock.com; p. 23 DeeaF/Shutterstock.com.

Printed in the United States of America

CPSIA compliance information: Batch #CW17GS: For further information contact Gareth Stevens, New York, New York at 1-800-542-2595.